THE GHOSTLY TALES OF

VANCOUVER

Published by Arcadia Children's Books
A Division of Arcadia Publishing, Inc.
Charleston, SC
www.arcadiapublishing.com

Spooky America is a trademark of Arcadia Publishing, Inc.

First published 2024
Manufactured in the United States

Designed by Jessica Nevins
Images used courtesy of Shutterstock.com; p. 46 jejim/Shutterstock.com; p. 55 Library
of Congress Prints and Photographs Division Washington, D.C. 20540 USA/LC-BH826-
3703 [P&P]; p. 64 NPS; pp. 68-69 Edward Cochrane, Navy Department, Bureau of
Ships/File:13-2-3 Oregon-SB-Portland-25.jpg/Wikimedia Commons/ Public domain.

ISBN: 978-1-4671-9772-4
Library of Congress Control Number: 2024931209

Spooky America

THE
GHOSTLY TALES
OF
VANCOUVER

DAN ALLEVA

Adapted from Haunted Vancouver, Washington by Pat Jollota

arcadia
CHILDREN'S BOOKS

WASHINGTON

OREGON

IDAHO

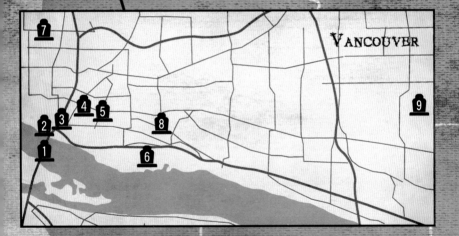

VANCOUVER

7

4 5

2 3

8

1

9

6

NEVADA

CALIFORNIA

TABLE OF CONTENTS & MAP KEY

Fort Vancouver

Welcome to Spooky Vancouver!

Along the banks of the Columbia River lies Vancouver, Washington, the oldest city in the state—and possibly its most HAUNTED!

This region of the Pacific Northwest has a rich history. At one time, the Chinook Nation called this frontier its home. These Indigenous people were strong fighters and skilled elk and salmon hunters. In 1805 and 1806, the renowned explorers Lewis and Clark sailed along this area on the Columbia River during their exploration of the American West.

In 1824, the Hudson's Bay Company— North America's oldest merchant of goods— established Fort Vancouver, where the Columbia and Willamette Rivers meet. It served as the headquarters of the company's successful fur trade in the area. Furs and other goods were sent down the rivers. As business grew, the Oregon Trail branched off to end at the fort as a place where people could pick up supplies.

In 1846, a treaty made Washington a part of the United States. And in 1849, the

U.S. Army arrived and built what is now the oldest American military installation in the Pacific Northwest. Many brave soldiers have made their way to combat from Vancouver's shores. It's natural to assume that many never returned, but that doesn't mean the spirits of those soldiers didn't find their way back to the banks of the Columbia River.

The City of Vancouver was finally incorporated on January 23, 1857. What was once an early settlement in the area that thrived on fishing and the fur trade is now a bustling city with a population of around 200,000 people. And Vancouver's rich history

Fort Vancouver

has prompted historians to call the city, "One place across time."

So, is it really that strange to think such a notable city and "place across time" could be in the grips of supernatural energy? What about the terrifying presence people often feel when traveling along Vancouver's Interstate Bridge?

This bridge is such a matter of intrigue in Vancouver because it is no stranger to tragic occurrences. Men have crossed the bridge never to return alive again. Foolish showboats thinking they were courageous have plunged from its edges only to meet their certain death. There's also the small matter of a plane that crashed and burned against the bridge's towering pillars, killing the pilot.

How about the ghost that resides in Room 160 of the Thunderbird Inn at the Quay? If you're unsure if ghosts are truly real, just ask the good folks at the Thunderbird what they believe. They will tell you of a Vancouver woman named Marcia Patterson who tragically died at the hands of her own husband. Now, she haunts the cold confines of Room 160, scaring the daylights out of anyone who stays inside.

But don't shudder these pages closed in a hurry just yet. Whether we call it a spirit or manifestation, ghosts aren't always bad (but when they are, it's never good!). So, we must be cautious along the way. Now, if you're ready, how about we pop in on some of the phantasms that call Vancouver home?

The Interstate Bridge

A Bridge Like No Other

Today, there are approximately 600,000 major bridges across the United States. They all make it possible for people to travel along the roads and highways that crisscross this country, eventually making it to their final destination. One such bridge is in Vancouver—the Interstate Bridge. Commonly known as the I-5 Bridge, it's also called the Vancouver-Portland Bridge, as it connects these two cities across the Columbia River.

But this is no ordinary bridge. It has been the scene of bizarre disappearances, deadly displays of courage, and—oh yeah—a PLANE CRASH. There is no doubt that the Interstate Bridge is well known for its very strange history!

Construction of the Interstate Bridge first began in 1915, and by 1917, the northbound lane from Portland to Vancouver was complete. Later, the southbound lane was constructed, and soon after, a lane of tracks for freight rail was also added. The bridge stretches 3,500 feet

(about the size of a professional soccer field), transporting as many as 130,000 vehicles between Vancouver and Portland each day. However, one patron of the bridge is most peculiar—because there's a good chance he's actually quite dead!

Many have reported seeing a tall, slender man in a fedora hat and overcoat walking along the bridge. If you see this man, he'll likely be gone in a flash, as he seems uninterested in interacting with passersby. Johanna, a resident of Vancouver, came close to meeting the mystery man. She spotted him as she walked across the bridge one night, but he vanished into the dark after she greeted him.

The leading theory of who this shadowy figure is traces its roots all the way back to October 17, 1920, when Mayor Grover Percival presided over Vancouver. On Election Night of 1920, Mayor Percival walked off on his own and was last seen heading for the bridge. When he didn't return, a search party was organized to locate him, but they had no luck. A month later, a hunter discovered the mayor's body on nearby Hayden Island, a small sliver of land with an eastern shoreline that runs underneath the Interstate Bridge. It appeared Mayor Percival had hanged himself—with his own handkerchief, in fact.

But those who knew Mayor Percival well had a hard time believing he had taken his own life. For one thing, hanging oneself with a handkerchief seemed an unlikely, if not impossible, thing to do. For another, the mayor had not seemed under any emotional stress. He had not chosen to run for re-election and appeared happy his good friend, John P. Kiggins, had just won the election to be Vancouver's next mayor. Finally, Mayor Percival had not left a note for his loved ones to say goodbye and explain why he had decided to end his life. The more people thought about it, the more they began to suspect something more sinister at play. Could Mayor Percival have been . . . murdered?

And if so, *why*?

The answer might have something to do with the Interstate Bridge. Despite the many advantages the bridge presented to the entire Pacific Northwest, there were some people who were angry that it had been built. They had even filed lawsuits to block its construction. When the Governor of Washington had refused to fund the project, two counties— Multnomah County in Vancouver and Clark County in Washington—raised the funds and built the bridge without any government funding. This had made some people even angrier, causing the mood among the communities on either side of the river to become quite tense.

Mayor Grover Percival had been a major player in organizing fundraising for the bridge. With tempers at a boiling point, could an angry citizen have followed Percival across the bridge, killed him, and then staged his death to appear as a suicide on Hayden Island? It's surely possible, though the only thing regional historians seem to agree on is that we'll likely never know what happened to Mayor Percival.

Percival wouldn't be the last person to spend their final moments on the Interstate Bridge. In 1934, death came calling for Roland McCall, who fancied himself as a bit of a daredevil. During a July 4 water show, he dove off the bridge, thinking he could survive the 110-foot plunge into the river. Regrettably, he thought wrong. It also took a full month before authorities fished McCall's corpse from the deep waters. But as foolish as McCall's bravery was, far more frightening are the sounds of a mysterious airplane that can be heard overhead at night, but never seen by a living soul in Vancouver. This unsettling story dates back to 1928, when a small plane valiantly fought the elements while searching for its landing spot at the Portland Airport, a new facility near the Interstate Bridge on Swan Island.

Pilot Clarence Price faced a dilemma as he flew through the skies one foggy November night. Price, who learned to be a pilot while serving in World War I, was now an airmail delivery man, flying mail from region to region. But on that fateful evening, Price was unable to locate the airport due to the thick fog.

Cruising at a low altitude, Price circled above the area, flying back and forth over the Columbia River. As the fog worsened, he struggled to spot the two markers he'd made for himself just below: Swan Island to the west, and Camus, a town along the coastline of Washington just to the east of Vancouver. Growing frantic, Price had no choice but to cruise down to an even lower altitude of just fifty feet above the water. He circled over Camus once more, hoping to find *anywhere* to land.

As his plane sped through the thick and merciless fog, Price must have thought he

was high enough to clear the 110-foot cement block counterweights of the Interstate Bridge. But he got the trajectory wrong. Moments later, his plane crashed into the bridge's north tower, plummeted to the lumberyard below, and burst into flames. Though people rushed to the scene and tried to pull Price to safety, he did not survive the fiery crash.

To this day, there are some people who believe Price's plane—and the sound of his screams—can be heard at night, circling east to west and back again between Swan Island and Camus. Once, a bartender at Warehouse 23, a restaurant located underneath the Interstate Bridge, sensed a commotion in the sky. The man was just about to close the bar for the evening, when he suddenly heard what he later described as "a scream of horror and agony" echoing in the night sky. The bartender quickly locked the restaurant doors and ran for safety. Was it Pilot Price again, still looking for his final destination? Who can say, really? More disturbing, though, are the events that followed in the wake of the tragedy.

Not long after, mail that Price was carrying onboard was retrieved from the crash site and delivered to a Portland newspaper. Among its contents was a photo, charred around the edges from the blast. It was the image of a similar plane that had suffered the exact same fate only a week before on Long Island, New York. Was the photo's arrival at the newspaper simply a coincidence, or could Price have actually been carrying cursed cargo onboard with him? Again, we can't truly know—but when in Vancouver, it's worth remembering to pause for a moment and listen to the wind. You may just hear the engines of a plane piloted by none other than the ghost of Clarence Price.

The Saga of the Thunderbird Inn

The winds of the Pacific Northwest were ripping through the downtown streets of Vancouver with savage force. Ice had blanketed nearly every road possible. The owners of the Thunderbird Inn at the Quay, concerned for the safety of their employees, begged the staff to stay at the inn for the night. The staff were grateful: no one was looking forward to the treacherous drive home. By nightfall, each of the staff members had settled into their rooms for the night.

Room 160, however, remained empty, for not a soul would dare sleep a single second within its four walls. After all, the staff knew all too well what had happened inside. While many believe Vancouver to be crawling with poltergeists (spirits known for physical disturbances or unexplained noises), no one has made *more* appearances, so to speak, than the woman who haunts Room 160 at the Thunderbird Inn.

The apparition, presumed to be a woman named Marcia Patterson, was first discovered by a housekeeper at the inn. Working her way through the rooms before check-in, the housekeeper entered Room 160 one morning, surprised to find a woman sitting on the bed.

"Oh, excuse me!" said the

housekeeper, so shocked at first glance, she quickly stepped back and closed the door. After taking a moment to collect her thoughts, she reentered the room, intending to find out if the woman needed anything. But the woman was gone. She had totally vanished. The housekeeper could only stand awestruck in the doorway. How could this be? Could the housekeeper's mind have been playing tricks on her? Naturally, that was *one* possibility.

It wasn't until a couple from California, visiting Vancouver on holiday, had a similar encounter. After drifting in and out of deep sleep for hours, the husband suddenly woke up. His eyes widened just long enough to see the figure of a woman, shimmering in a garment made of glitter. As soon as the man reached for the lamp and lit the room to see who—or *what*—stood before him, the figure was gone. Just as had happened to the housekeeper. But who was this mystery woman? That morning at breakfast, the man recalled to the waiter his strange encounter from the night before.

"Ah, you must be staying in Room 160," the waiter said. By now, it seemed everyone at the Thunderbird Inn knew about this strange woman who appeared and vanished in the blink of an eye. Intrigued, the man and his wife traveled to the library with hopes of learning more about who she might have been, and what may have happened at the Thunderbird Inn. This is how the story of Marcia Patterson became legendary in Vancouver.

The year was 1975. Marcia was once married to a man named Jackie Charles Patterson. Jackie was known for having a relaxed, nonchalant personality. He had a crooked smile and walked with a limp. But there was something peculiar about him—beginning with his marriage to Marcia. While she lived in the McLoughlin Heights section of Vancouver, Jackie lived nearly 1,500 miles away in Arizona.

Strange as this was, the distance was nothing compared to the mind games Jackie played on Marcia. He, rather smugly, would rip a $100 bill in half, then mail one half of the bill to Marcia in Vancouver. What was his point in doing this?

Well, when Jackie wanted to see his wife, he presumed the worst in her, and assumed she'd come running for the other half of the $100 bill. Worse still, Jackie would do this regularly. Can you even imagine such spitefulness, let alone accept it yourself? I should say not, and Marcia wasn't going to stand for it, either. One day, instead of receiving notice of Marcia's pending visit, Jackie received paperwork for divorce!

Soon after, Jackie took the train from Arizona all the way to Vancouver, with the intent of meeting with Marcia to ... work out their differences. At first, he stopped at a roadside motel and checked into a room. But, practically as soon as he checked in, he checked out. Why, may you wonder? Could it have been this room didn't have all the amenities Jackie needed—such as a motel set far back along the road, with a room at the rear, nearby an exit into the parking lot?

As in ... *an exit to carry a body out of?!*

Jackie found everything he needed and more at the Thunderbird Inn. He gathered his personal belongings and settled into—you guessed it—Room 160.

Meanwhile, Marcia was preparing to meet Jackie for dinner, to tell him face-to-face that she was leaving him and their marriage was done for good. She dressed in fine evening wear—a shimmering gown—and wore a wig, which was a fashionable thing to do at the time.

That evening, Jackie and Marcia dined together at a restaurant, where those who saw them said their meeting seemed cordial. But apparently, things started to go very wrong once Jackie and Marcia returned to the Thunderbird Inn. The pair began to argue about the divorce. Allegedly, Jackie then forcefully pressed a pillow against Marcia's chest to muzzle the sound of the two bullets he fired into her heart! Marcia was killed instantly.

Jackie proceeded to wrap his wife's corpse in blankets and towels he gathered from the motel room. He carried her body through the back of the Thunderbird, out the rear entrance, and to the trunk of his car, where he placed her lifeless remains. Jackie returned to Room 160 one last time—to retrieve the wig that Marcia had been wearing. He threw that in the trunk, too, then began to drive away.

Jackie drove aimlessly through the night, now quite scared by what he had done. In a

panic, he called his sister, who desperately tried to convince Jackie to turn himself in to the authorities. So the following day, that's exactly what he did. Though, when the police arrived to meet him at the corner of Fifth and Main Streets, they noticed that Jackie wasn't exactly in his right mind—nor was he totally truthful at first with the officers. He told them, rather bizarrely, that his wife was in the trunk, and that he was "waiting for her to knock to be let out." As strange as it sounds to us now, imagine how the policemen felt!

When they finally opened the trunk of Jackie's car, they found Marcia's lifeless body, tossed in the trunk with barely a care, and her wig still beside her. The authorities quickly handcuffed Jackie and placed him under arrest.

One would think this incident spelled curtains for Mr. Jackie Charles Patterson, but sadly, it did not. What troubled investigators most was that not much of a crime scene was left in Room 160. Strangely enough, housekeeping had already cleaned up the room by the time police arrived to investigate. Bloody bedding and other bath items sat in the laundry room of the Thunderbird. What housekeeping had assumed happened inside, one couldn't possibly imagine. But it is worth remembering no one heard Patterson's gun, thanks to his shots being muzzled by the pillow he thrust upon Marcia's chest. Worse still, the police had no one's version of the crime but Jackie's. There were no other witnesses, and it was certainly too late to ask Marcia for a statement!

From the beginning, it seemed like justice for Marcia was uncertain. Jackie's sister testified on her brother's behalf at his trial, claiming that when Jackie was born, he was deprived oxygen to his brain, which would result in him making bad decisions throughout life. And as for Jackie? Well, he maintained his innocence, claiming that the whole affair was a tragic accident.

Jackie admitted he and Marcia had returned to the Thunderbird Inn and argued about the divorce. At one point, Jackie became frustrated and began to fire his pistol, something he said "he did regularly" as a way to relax. In fact, he'd told police, "I like to shoot holes in things." Marcia, Jackie claimed, had been struck by accident.

Shooting holes in things? Inside a motel room? To relax?! *Really?* Nonetheless, Jackie was found not guilty. The jury did not believe that prosecutors had provided enough evidence to convict Jackie, and he was set free. Now, the

spirit of Marcia Paterson lingers in Room 160, perhaps a result of her being denied the justice she deserved.

But Marcia didn't die in vain. Though it took a while, justice finally caught up to Jackie Patterson. After departing Vancouver a free man, Jackie relocated to Oklahoma, where a brazen pattern of violence followed him. Women acquainted with him disappeared mysteriously, or worse, had his will imposed upon them physically. Jackie had also by now

married a second woman named Cynthia. Soon enough, Cynthia went missing, too. The authorities found Cynthia's body buried under a concrete slab in Jackie's yard. He knew he'd finally come to the end of the road, and he couldn't outrun the police any longer. He fired a shotgun blast straight to his head before he could be apprehended.

An ironic ending for a man who enjoyed making holes in things, wouldn't you say?

Fraud, Guns, and Ghosts

At first glance, the glass studio that sits at the corner of Main Street and Fifth doesn't seem all that mysterious. But if you knew of the strange happenings there and in the neighboring buildings, you may think twice about what your eyes truly see.

The glass studio is connected to what used to be the Evergreen Hotel, which was known for its popular ballroom, Alexander's.

The Evergreen is no longer there today, nor is Alexander's, and in its place is now an assisted living facility. But off to the side is the glass studio, where many glass artists come to perfect their skills. The building is covered in terracotta tiles that were installed in 1926, and its beauty makes it quite the attraction in downtown Vancouver. However, it was not always a glass studio. In 1910, it was the First National Bank, with friends Charles Brown its president and E. L. Canby its cashier.

Charles Brown and E. L. Canby both came from prominent families. Canby was married to Frances Burnside. Both were descendants of original Oregon pioneers whose families had done very well for themselves. Charles Brown was the son of the dignified Samuel Brown, an original financier in Vancouver appointed to the position personally by President Abraham Lincoln.

Charles was married to Rebecca Slocum, who was also from a successful family with Vancouver roots. Together, they lived in a beautifully ornate and grand house built in 1886. Sitting on West Eleventh Street, it is one of the last Victorian homes standing in Vancouver. It also played a prominent role in Charles and Rebecca's life together: the couple was married there, their children were born in the house, and Charles even celebrated his election to the position of city councilman there.

Despite what seemed to be a prosperous, elite life the two families led in Vancouver, greed had consumed both Brown and Canby, and for their deceit, the two men paid the ultimate price.

One day, a bank examiner came to the First National

Bank. As he walked through its doors, Canby's spine went rigid. He was overcome with fear and dread. Canby knew what the examiner had come for. It seemed that suspicious activity at the First National Bank had come to the attention of the bank examiner. Questionable loans were being made, and there were suspicious accounting records from which one could only draw a single conclusion: fraud! Now, the examiner was at the bank, looking for answers, and he wanted them right there and then. What happened next set off a wave of tragedy that shocked Vancouver to its very core.

Canby—feeling the weight of his dubious deeds—panicked immediately. He grabbed a revolver from his desk drawer and ran through the bank and out the back door. Once outside, Canby pointed the weapon at his head and fired. But the gun jammed! Distraught, he moved to fire again, but before he could squeeze the trigger, Brown and the examiner appeared, dragging him back inside.

"We are caught, Charles," Canby said, grabbing Brown's hand. But Brown had other ideas. This time, *he* drew another pistol and pointed it straight at the bank examiner. Then, Brown and Canby fled on foot, heading north. They first made a stop to the Brown House on West Eleventh Street. As Brown was leaving, he stood in the doorway for a moment, feeling the unbearable weight of cowardice bearing down on his shoulders.

They were determined to never be taken alive. They next ran for over a mile before reaching a field located at what is now

Thirty-Ninth and Kaufman Streets. Standing in the middle of the field, Canby began scrawling a note to his wife, asking for her forgiveness and pleading with her to take care of their children. He then raised a gun to his head for a second time that afternoon and fired. This time it didn't jam, and Canby fell lifeless to the ground. Brown followed, taking his own life using the very same pistol, and collapsing over his dead friend. Their doomed flight from justice had ended tragically.

Today, workers at the glass studio say they often feel a strange presence, as if someone is watching over them. But workers don't seem to mind. In fact, one artist proclaimed rather happily that the ghosts are "why I'm here!" Have Charles Brown and E. L. Canby come back to the place they knew so well, their guilty spirits trapped in ghostly limbo?

What do *you* think it could be?

But wait! There's more paranormal activity happening at the Brown House. Today, the building is home to a law office, but workers

there say they can feel the presence of a spirit hovering over them as they work.

Since Charles did briefly stop here before taking his own life, it is possible he is haunting both the glass factory and his former home. Ghosts have been known to haunt multiple locations and are not always confined to a single place or tied to certain events. Paranormal experts don't have a reasoning for this phenomenon, only suggesting that ghostly

energy has the ability to, well ... wander, you could say!

Just what we needed, right? A ghost on the move, as if ghosts aren't tricky enough to track in one spot!

Ulysses S. Grant House

Hauntings Inside
the Grant House

What if there was an entire stretch of land that was so haunted, just the thought of the madness found there would keep anyone lying awake at night? Naturally, we're talking about the 680-acre area inside Vancouver's city center known as Officers Row. In fact, many locals have rightfully crowned this entire area of Clark County the most haunted spot in Vancouver.

Aside from being *totally* haunted, Officers Row is also known for its large estate homes belonging to the very affluent Vancouver citizens. Vancouver has changed a lot through the years, so it's understandable how an integral section of town can change with it.

But one famed building—the Grant House— still remains at the heart of Officers Row. Today, the Grant House is a popular local eatery. Yet it seems that no matter what becomes of the Grant House, the overwhelming amount of paranormal activity happening there remains the same: it's off the charts!

When the United States military arrived in Washington in 1849, soldiers built what became some of the first long-standing structures within Vancouver. At first, they stayed in homes that had already been constructed by the Hudson's Bay Company. But there wasn't enough housing for all the men stationed there, so nine log homes were built to accommodate the men who needed beds. These houses were anything but luxurious and a far cry from anything you would see there today.

The wind would whip right through the structures, sometimes taking pieces of the building with it. One soldier remarked the homes were like "corrals with roofs on top of them."

In 1856, though, things got a little bit better for those staying at the Grant House. Weatherboarding, window, and door cases were added to the structure, which was more than likely a welcome addition for those living there. But one unfortunate soul who lived at the Grant House suffered a series of traumas and tragedy, until finally the harsh realities of life caught up with him.

General Alfred Sully was a commander in the U.S. Army who married the daughter of a Spanish nobleman, a beautiful young woman named Manuela. However, happiness was short-lived for the bliss-filled couple. Soon after Manuela and Alfred were married, a former admirer caught wind of their marriage. The man became so engulfed with envy and jealousy that he hatched a devious and deadly plot. He sent a fruit basket to Alfred and Manuela, who had recently given birth to the couple's first child. Little did they know of the teachery hidden within that basket: the fruit inside was poisoned. After eating an orange from the basket, Manuela fell sick and ultimately died. Sadly, her baby's fate, too, was short-lived. One evening not long after Manuela's death, the child's grandmother fell asleep with the infant still at her side. Tragically, she smothered the child.

After losing his beloved wife and baby, General Sully was never quite the same. Though he eventually remarried, the death of his first wife and child turned him mean and cruel, and his superiors often disciplined him for his behavior. By the time he was stationed in Vancouver along Officers Row at the Grant House, those within his ranks viewed it as a demotion.

Sully remained at Grant House until the end of his military career. As his health deteriorated and he was forced off the battlefield, Alfred Sully lived more and more in solitude. That is, until the summer of 1879, when something managed to garner the crack of a smile from General Sully.

Ulysses S. Grant was returning to Vancouver for a visit—this time as the former President of the United States. The famous general had gone on to serve as the eighteenth president of the nation from 1869 to 1877. A now-ecstatic Sully began preparing for the former president's visit, but alas, bad luck struck General Sully once again. After falling ill and suffering with stomach problems, Sully died on August 27, 1879. He missed Grant's visit by three months.

It's safe to say that luck or good fortune was probably never in the cards for General Sully. Now, his spirit is said to remain trapped inside the Grant House. Multiple times, paranormal experts have entered the Grant House to investigate. On one such visit to the house, a psychic came along as part of the investigation team. Believe it or not, a local television crew also joined the expedition, so they could document whatever might transpire inside.

The investigation was a disaster from the very beginning. First, the person with the keys to the house never showed up. Later, the crew experienced extreme technical difficulties. And once investigators finally got inside, the vibe was instantly unsettling. It would appear as though General Sully has taken his salty disposition with him into the afterlife!

Suzy Taylor, former owner of the restaurant

that is now in the Grant House, once saw a man she believes to have been Sully standing at the top of a staircase, very strangely out of place and of ill character. When she asked her staff who was upstairs, she was told no one was working above them. Funny as it may seem, Taylor was at ease. She'd finally caught the glimpse of an actual ghost!

Ulysses S. Grant

Marked by Murder

Would you be surprised to find out that ghosts have been living in the home you just moved into? What if they were *really strange* ghosts?!

That's exactly what happened to a tenant living in the side complex next to the Grant House along Officers Row. Most notably, there was something very unsettling about the upstairs bedroom. There was a stain on the floor that—no matter how it was cleaned, no matter how determined one was to remove it—would return again and again. It made the tenant feel uncomfortable, and to tell you the absolute truth, it makes me more than a bit uncomfortable, too!

Throwing rugs over the stain did nothing to hide the obvious: the stain was *still* there underneath, no matter what anybody did to ignore it. It was as if this mysterious mark enjoyed playing the role of tormentor! But as it turns out, this stain was no black magic at all. It was a reminder that death—especially by murder—can never be swept under the rug.

Inside the bedroom, complaints of a cold, strong breeze were quite common, despite no window or door being open. Some Vancouver locals believe this strong breeze might not be a breeze at all—but, rather, the restless spirit of a woman who once lived in the house named Sonia Petersen. In life, Sonia's family remembered her as a powerful woman of incredible resilience, as well as a devoted single mother. But sadly, as it would turn out, Sonia was also a woman who died of a broken heart.

When Sonia moved into the duplex with her young child, it was by the good grace of her friend Michelle Nagle, who gave Sonia shelter—at least for a short while. Michelle had a room in the front of the building, while Sonia kept quarters in a room to the back, with her child in the room next to her.

Although she'd lived through some struggles, Sonia finally met a man who might provide some stability. His name was Jeffrey Kern. He was handsome, charming, and quite taken with

Sonia. But it was all a terrible lie. Aside from being handsome and charming, Kern was also a criminal, wanted for burglary in another state and murder in another! Michelle Nagle, meanwhile, had a bad feeling about Kern from the beginning, and so she kept her eyes peeled for anything strange.

One Sunday evening, Michelle, Sonia, and her child had gone to sleep for the night, when a peculiar rustle awoke the two women. Someone had been roaming through the yard. Sonia called the police, but by the time the officers arrived at the scene, the alleged prowler had fled. This didn't stop Sonia from telling the authorities her hunch about who she believed had been creeping through their yard in the darkness: Jeffrey Kern.

The police were sympathetic, but without evidence or a motive as to why Kern would be prowling—and without Kern anywhere in sight—there was nothing they could do. After checking the property, the police left.

The officers had no way of knowing that they would be back the very next morning. Only this time, to everybody's horror, there would be no shortage of evidence. Sonia Petersen was murdered in her own bedroom, apparently from multiple stab wounds to the chest. She was found lying dead in her dress with her makeup complete, as though she were leaving for work. Michelle had found her in a pool of blood when Sonia hadn't arrived downstairs for breakfast as she normally would have. Kern was apprehended at once.

Is the bloodstained bedroom along Officers Row a crimson reminder that Sonia Peterson was once a person just like me and you, until her life was tragically—and savagely—cut short?

Only Sonia, wherever she is, can truly know for sure.

Kaiser Shipyard

The Gruesome Rise of the Kaiser Shipyard

It may be hard to imagine now, but Vancouver was once a quiet river town, not the busy and heavily populated city it is today. But a series of events changed that—and the future of Vancouver—forever.

The Japanese attack on Pearl Harbor on December 7, 1941 had decimated much of the existing U.S. Pacific Fleet and its headquarters, and the Pacific Ocean was vulnerable to enemy control. This attack is ultimately what pulled the United States into World War II.

Fortunately, the Kaiser Corporation and the Permanente Concrete Company stepped in to rebuild what had been destroyed—and rebuild in a hurry! The two corporations were very familiar with each other and with large scale construction. Together, they worked as partners to develop dams along the Columbia River prior to the start of the war. So, when the safety of the United States was seriously threatened, these two very capable businesses sprang into action, developing the Kaiser Shipyard.

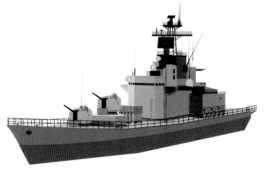

The shipyard was located on Ryan's Point, an area of land jutting out into the Columbia River, at the westernmost end. It was built in just six months, illustrating the urgency and severity of the situation. With the United States now drawn into World War II, filling manufacturing jobs was now a priority. Soon enough, Vancouver's population grew from about 8,500 people to nearly 90,000 practically overnight.

By July 1942, the yards were fully operational. The shipyard ran twenty-four hours a day, seven days a week, and its output of ships was done at a near breakneck speed. From the time a boat began construction to the time it set to sea took a meager seventy-two hours. Safety precautions were taken throughout the yard and the surrounding areas, but the workers there were desperate for time, and these new defenses came at an expense of

Shipyard in 1945

their own. Vancouver was expanding, and the city experienced many growing pains in the process.

The key issues were housing and transportation. With the wave of people coming into Vancouver, the city was not prepared in any way to provide such critical services. The I-5 bridge was jam-packed with traffic daily. So, to provide relief, travel vessels and tugboats were used to push or pull passenger boats across the Columbia River, between Vancouver and Portland. But these passenger boats were anything but sail-ready. Most of the time, they were just small ferry crafts with wooden benches attached to them. You'd really have to hold on to your hat while taking a trip on one of those boats, for sure!

The winter of 1943 was particularly cold, and most of the men who came to work in Vancouver were new recruits who brought their entire families with them. They were mostly from the Southern states, where the climate was much warmer and far more agreeable. Seldom were they prepared for the bitter temperatures, and when the cold hit, the men who worked in the shipyards, particularly, would be layered in almost anything they could find.

One freezing cold night, nineteen men boarded a vessel headed for Vancouver from Portland. But sadly, they never made it there. The icy river was choppy, and winds blew raw against the men's tired and weathered faces. Not long after departure, the boat capsized, killing ten of the nineteen people on board.

Many years later, a couple hiking along the Columbia River in Oregon came across a high levee, which is a raised bank or structure alongside a river that helps protect against floods. Once they had scaled their way to the top, they looked out onto the horizon, admiring the Washington coastline on the other side. But they were not prepared for what they saw next.

In the distance, they saw what appeared to be a boat. Only, it was not of the time period, and it looked like a combination of a tugboat and ferry boat. But before they could really get a fix on the craft, it was suddenly gone— as if it had vanished into thin air. When they returned to the city square, they paid a visit to the library to see if the area viewed from atop the levee had a history. There in the library, they learned the tragic story of the shipyard men who met a watery grave.

Could it be the couple had seen the infamous boat along the Columbia that fateful afternoon? It is possible, but then again, our eyes do have a habit of playing tricks on us. That said, if you're along the Vancouver riverside at any point, keep your eyes peeled for the phantom boat carrying nineteen sullen spirits.

In fact, if you look closely enough, you may just spot *another* wandering spirit along the banks of the Columbia. After all, while the shipyards were a big part of Vancouver's growth and prosperity, they were also a source of ghosts that continue to haunt the city.

By 1943, the war was beginning to wind down, and there was less need for so many ships. The yards began to close down elements

of operation, and many of the men faced layoffs. Losing one's job is hard enough, but the Kaiser Corporation was also one of the first companies in the United States to offer its employees modern health insurance. This meant shipyard workers could afford important medical care for themselves and their families—a revolutionary idea at the time! However, this made layoffs even more heartbreaking and stressful—not only would you lose your job, you'd lose your family's health insurance, too.

Sadly, this might help explain the terrible actions of one such shipyard employee: a man who lost his job with Kaiser . . . and then maybe lost his mind.

No one could ever piece together the man's motive, but one day, his wife awoke from a nap on their sofa to find her husband standing over her with an axe! She screamed as he swung downward repeatedly. Hearing the sound of their mother's screams, the couple's children ran into the room. When they saw everything covered in blood, the children ran in horror for safety to a neighbor's home. Sensing the end was near, the husband grabbed his pistol. In what may have been a final act of rage and frustration, he shot himself right there beside his wife.

When authorities arrived, they were aghast at the blood-splattered crime scene. Some of the men needed to step away to collect themselves before they could return to their work. When authorities later questioned the woman next door, she was reported as saying, "He was a good man, the shipyards ruined him."

The house has long since returned to a single-family dwelling. But ever since that day, on the second floor and in the attic, residents have talked of sudden gusts of frigid air, as well as moans heard faintly in the room. Old-timers on the street nod and whisper that it's the shipyard worker and his family reliving that awful night. Or maybe, it's just the sound of a creaky old house, moaning and groaning in the wind.

Whatever you believe, one thing is clear: a city's growth and change is rarely, if ever, smooth sailing. And sometimes, for better or worse, progress can leave all *kinds* of everlasting traces behind . . .

The Mummy in
the Bedroom

On the west side of Vancouver, there sits an unassuming, small house, set back from the road and shaded by trees. Built in the 1940s, the house is typical of its time: a small porch leads to a front door with a fireplace off to one side. The home's original owners were fairly unassuming, as well. The husband was a state tax commissioner, and his wife worked at home. Through the years, many people have lived in the house, but odd occurrences began to happen not long after one tenant moved in.

The tenant told paranormal investigators that she *was sure* there were two ghosts living in the home, one definitely being a female spirit. But that was only half the story. Household items would appear in completely random places. Paper goods for the bathroom would end up near the living room fireplace; small bedroom items would appear on the dining room table; and thumping and rattling noises could be heard throughout the house.

Any of these might send a person running for the hills, but only one thing truly scared the tenant: water would appear *everywhere*, for no apparent reason. Empty bowls inside cabinets would be filled mysteriously. The tenant would climb into bed at night only to discover that sheets underneath dry blankets and comforters were somehow soaked.

Through a series of research efforts, paranormal investigators were able to *dig up* information, you could say, on a curious couple who had once lived in the house.

Donald and Gwynn Layne were known by most of their neighbors as normal people. Don worked in tool repair and liked to talk about politics. Gwynn was ever-so-dedicated to the couple's home garden. Don had emphysema, a condition of the lungs, so he often took long naps while recovering from complications and generally stayed inside.

In December 1993, neighbors started to notice they hadn't seen Gwynn in her garden recently, which was out of character for her. She usually spent hours tending to flowers, petal by petal, nearly every day. So, when she wasn't seen for a week, it was peculiar. Out of concern for her safety, neighbors asked authorities to enter the home to check that Gwynn was okay.

After breaking through the front window, authorities found Gwynn lying on the floor. She had fallen and was unable to move. Medical officers tended to Gwynn while police began to observe the home. The place was in total shambles. Old magazines and newspapers were scattered about. Cobwebs lined the ceiling

from end to end, and large spiders hung from them like guardians of the domain.

Based on their estimations, paramedics could tell that Gwynn had been on the floor for nearly a week. She had no food or water, and she was badly dehydrated.

A medic then asked Gwynn if she lived in the house alone.

"No, my husband is here, too," she said.

The medics all looked at each other, puzzled. If someone else was home, how had Gwynn been on the floor for days?

"Where is he, ma'am? Is he okay?" asked one medic.

"Oh, he's about the same," said Gwynn. "He's over in the bedroom."

In the bedroom, the paramedics discovered something from a horror movie. They found what remained of Donald Layne: his corpse was completely mummified!

Detectives soon pieced the story together. Donald had gone to lie down one day to take a nap, but he likely never made it to the bedroom. He must have died suddenly making his way there. When Gwynn found Don, she went into a state of shock. So, she moved him to the bedroom, covered him with a blanket, and shut the door. *For an entire year.*

Inside Donald's pants pocket was a newspaper clipping for a speaking engagement he might have been thinking about attending, helping the police pinpoint the time and cause of death.

Most people in Vancouver know the story of the Mummy of Lavina, as Donald is now known. It's assumed that both Gwynn and

Donald haunt the house today. But what is the significance of the water, you ask? Paranormal researchers haven't been able to come up with a conclusive answer. Some believe the bowls of water represent the days of thirst Gwynn endured while her husband lie mummified in his bedroom—but this is merely speculation.

What do you think? Do you have any idea what soggy tricks Gwynn and Donald might be up to? Until someone does, it shall remain a matter of debate in Vancouver.

Forgotten Graves

What would you do if you found out your house was built on top of a former graveyard? Would you leave? Or would you be practical about it, even if you did want some answers? Those are both reasonable reactions, I suppose. But what if you learned that contractors forgot to move a couple of the graves—and the accompanying bodies—before building the homes? Well, I don't know about you, but I saw a movie about this very sort of thing, and it did not end well! So, I would be out of there in a hurry. The same can be said for many people who've called stretches of Edgewood in Vancouver their homes.

In the early 1930s, local government thought building a mausoleum (a memorial building for the dead) along the Columbia River was a fantastic idea. The plan was for loved ones to pay their respects to the dead while taking in the scenic riverfront for comfort. It

was a well-intentioned idea, of course. But by the time the Great Depression was in full swing, there was no money available to complete the memorial, and so the mausoleum project was abandoned.

Now, this is where things got dicey for the folks living near Edgewood!

At the beginning of the project, a temporary mausoleum was built to hold the remains of the dead, intended only for a short period before the finished design could be completed. But once the mausoleum project was abandoned, the temporary crypt became all but a distant memory. Over time, the coffins were exposed as the structure began to deteriorate. When three high school kids took a corpse in their car for a joyride around town before throwing it into a lake, the town finally took some action. Eventually, most of the bodies were transferred to more suitable grounds throughout Vancouver.

I say *most* bodies, because in the end, not every poor soul could be accounted for. Record keeping was sketchy at best. One woman opened a coffin expecting to find her teenage son but instead found the startling remains of a balding, middle-aged man. By time the land was sold off, no one could honestly say for sure if the entire area was cleared of bodies.

With time, houses were built on the former mausoleum site. One summer, a man living in one of the homes noticed that his garden hose would mysteriously move all around his front lawn. No matter where he left it, when he returned later in the day, the hose would be in a completely different place. This became an issue, as brown spots began to appear across his front lawn. With no obvious explanation, the man shared his bizarre garden hose story with his neighbor. Sure enough, the neighbor next door was experiencing the same thing! The man was stunned. How was this even possible? After all, a garden hose can't just pick up and move by itself!

And yet . . . that's exactly what happened.

One day, convinced that some small animal had been toying with the hose while his back was turned, the man set it out on his lawn just as he normally would. Only *this* time, he hid on his porch and waited. The man waited for quite a while, but he was determined to put an end to the madness before it drove him mad, too!

Then, suddenly, the phone inside the house began to ring. Without rising from his lookout spot on the porch, the man glanced toward the front door. The phone rang once and stopped. He couldn't have taken his eye off the hose for longer than a millisecond—and yet, when he turned back around, it had moved! The man stood in disbelief and could not explain what he'd just seen—or *hadn't* seen, to be precise.

Had ghostly remains of the abandoned mausoleum used their psychic capabilities to make the phone ring, diverting the man's attention just long enough to move the hose? No one can say for sure, but I imagine the man left the gardening to the ghosts from that point on. After all, they were there first!

CHAPTER 9

The Life and Death of Louis Boucher

On the east side of Vancouver, an elderly man was deathly afraid to return to his home one evening. Neighbors could see the fear on the man's face, and it was an uncomfortable sight to bear. He had once been a strong, adventurous, successful young man—before everything was pulled out from underneath him like a rug. Now, he was standing before his neighbors, pleading for help. They didn't know at the time that he would soon be dead. The man's name was Louis D. Boucher, and his murder remains unpunished to this very day.

Many of Vancouver's neighborhoods have evolved since the late 1930s and 1940s. However, at Vancouver's Historic Museum, arial photos from that time show that Vancouver's east side was largely taken up by farms and orchards, as far as the eye could see. At the time, this area was known as the Burton District.

Old Burton District documents and photos show there once existed a very small home

on a farm of only ten acres—unusual given the large farms and fields that surround it. If you weren't searching for it, the home would be hard to find. Nonetheless, it came to the attention of paranormal investigators when its current owners reported strange occurrences inside, such as objects crashing to the floor unexpectedly, and doors thrown wide open with gigantic clatter. As investigators soon learned, this was once the home of Louis Boucher.

Louis was involved with several professional endeavors throughout his life, and he was a bit of a proud man. He told his neighbors in Vancouver that he had owned a copper mine in the Southwest. He also told people that he owned his own scenic trail inside the Grand Canyon, called the Boucher Trail. He had allegedly arrived in Arizona in 1891, buying several properties and lands in the surrounding areas. He kept the deeds to these lands in his pocket to prove they were really his.

After an active, if not simple, life near the Grand Canyon, Louis got the sense that his days of adventure were catching up with him. Retirement was calling. So, he decided to move to Vancouver to live out the rest of his days near his sister, a nun who lived in Clark County. Louis ultimately settled into the house on the small piece of farmland in the Burton District.

By this time, Louis was more than ninety years old. In order to maintain the income and quality of life he enjoyed, Louis signed his land over to a man named Leon Jones, on the condition that Louis could remain in his humble home while Jones took care of the farm. This agreement worked well for both men at first—but it was short lived.

Leon began to grow tired of the agreement he'd made with Louis. He felt the land could be more valuable to him if he could just sell it. So, without letting Louis know of his plans, Leon sold the house to a man named Fred Jones— no relation of Leon's—who swore he would maintain the agreement that Louis had made with Leon. While he might have been tired of running the farm, Leon didn't want any harm to come to Louis as he enjoyed the twilight of his life.

What Leon didn't realize, unfortunately, was that Fred Jones was a liar. Fred figured that, at Louis's age, he'd hardly have to wait long for Louis to die. Then, he could fully claim the farm and all that came with it for himself. But what *Fred* didn't know was that despite Louis's age, he was fit as a fiddle and as sharp as a tack! As far as Louis was concerned, he wasn't going anywhere, *anytime* soon. He was incensed when he learned that Leon Jones had sold the farm without telling him, and he sought to take both Leon and Fred to court to reclaim his land. But unfortunately, the court never heard Louis's case.

The day after Louis was seen pleading with his neighbors for help, Fred Jones reported to authorities that Louis Bouchard had gone missing. Fred suggested that Louis was suffering from dementia and had most likely run off and gotten lost in the middle of the night. But the people of the Burton District weren't buying that story. Louis had already told his neighbors about the physical abuse he had suffered at the hands of Fred, who wanted

him gone from the land. The townspeople suspected foul play.

It wasn't until mid-July—nearly three weeks since Louis's disappearance—that his body floated to the surface of the Columbia River, his own clothesline knotted tightly around his neck. Authorities pieced together the crime, presuming the assailant had attacked Louis in his home while he slept in his evening chair, choking him to death from behind.

They arrested Fred Jones on July 18, alleging he had the motive and means to kill Louis Boucher and dispose of his body. A trial was set for Halloween, but Fred's defense attorneys pushed for a mistrial, claiming the time limit to prosecute Fred had expired. The judge agreed. According to Washington law, Fred Jones needed to be brought before a jury by October 18, and no later. The judge dismissed the charges immediately, and Jones was set free.

To add insult to injury, Fred Jones fled Vancouver. But he continued to commit ghastly crimes and escape punishment. This pattern continued until he, too, disappeared, never to be heard from again. Could he possibly have fled to poor Louis's Grand Canyon retreat? Or maybe somebody along the way had taken justice into their own hands and made Fred Jones disappear for good!

With time and innovation, it's possible investigators will one day piece together the truth surrounding this terrible tragedy. For now, nearly one hundred years later, true and fair justice still evades Louis Boucher. As for

the ghostly disturbances Louis is likely causing, perhaps he's simply grown tired of waiting for someone to solve his murder. And maybe all the commotion he's creating inside his former home is his way of urging people on.

A Ghostly Goodbye

Now that you've learned about some of Vancouver's ghostly gravesites and grisly tragedies, what do you think? Can unfinished business in this life lead to limbo in the afterlife? It makes you wonder, doesn't it? What *really* happened to the spirits of Marcia Patterson and Louis Boucher after they'd been outmuscled and overmatched by death? And what of their tormentors who seemingly got away with their crimes? Perhaps they received a punishment of their own once they reached the great beyond? Truth be told, your informed opinion is the only one that matters here.

However, the next time you visit Vancouver, be sure to look over your shoulder when you walk the streets and keep an eye open while

you're sleeping—there may just be someone hovering over you with an axe!

That is, of course . . . if you're now willing to believe it's possible.

Dan Alleva is an author from Brooklyn, New York. When not writing, Dan can be found rooting on his beloved Manchester United with his incredible daughter, Olivia Jane.

Check out some of the other *Spooky America* titles available now!

Spooky America was adapted from the creeptastic *Haunted America* series for adults. *Haunted America* explores historical haunts in cities and regions across America. Here's more from the original *Haunted Vancouver, Washington* author, Pat Jollota: